not a guide to

Harrogate & District

Trish Colton

THE TEWIT WELL

THE CHALYBEATE SPRING BENEATH THIS TEMPLE IS BELIEVED TO HAVE BEEN DISCOVERED BY WILLIAM SLINGSBY IN 1571 AND IS THE OLDEST KNOWN SPRING IN HARROGATE.
THE PRESENT COVER WAS BUILT FROM DESIGNS BY THOMAS CHIPPINDALE IN 1807-8 AND UP TO 1842 STOOD OVER THE SULPHUR SPRING IN LOW HARROGATE.

THE HARROGATE SOCIETY, 1975

First published 2012

The History Press
The Mill, Brimscombe Port
Stroud, Gloucestershire, GL5 2QG
www.thehistorypress.co.uk

British Library Cataloguing in Publication Data.
A catalogue record for this book is available from the British Library.

ISBN 978 0 7524 7655 1

Typesetting and origination by The History Press
Printed in Great Britain

Coat of Arms

Harrogate's original coat of arms was granted in 1884 and represented the history of the spa. The new coat of arms for Harrogate was granted in 1974 and represents various parts of the district.

*

The ears of wheat and Ribston Pippin apple tree indicate the large rural areas.

*

The four quarters contain the White Rose of Yorkshire, the horn of Ripon, the mineral springs of Harrogate and the ancient castle of Knaresborough.

*

The wavy lines depict the several rivers which run through the district.

*

The original motto was *Arx Celebris Fontibus* – a city famous for its springs. The new motto is, 'To be of Service'.

Contents

What's in a Name?

Harrogate was originally known as Bilton-with-Harrogate. Bilton's name can be traced back to AD 972 and it is mentioned in the Domesday survey.

There are a variety of meanings on offer for the name Harrogate. Take your choice from:

Grey hill road

The road to the hill of the soldier

The road to the cairn

The names of nearby towns also have intriguing meanings:

Boroughbridge: Bridge near the stronghold, or new town on the bridge.

Knaresborough: Stronghold of a man called Cenheard.

Masham: Homestead or village of a man called Mæssa.

Pateley Bridge: Woodland clearing near the paths.

Ripon: (Place in the territory of) the tribe called Hrype.

Grid Reference

Betty's Café Tea Rooms, 1 Parliament Street

SE 30096 55294

Latitude: 53.992851

Longitude: -1.5425310

Strange Street Names

There are some wonderful street names both in Harrogate itself and in the district. But sometimes there's less of a mystery to these names than might at first appear. 'Haywra' simply meant the track to the hayfield; Barefoot Street probably had more to do with acts of penance by erring Christian pilgrims on their way to Ripon Cathedral than with the poor of the city.

Romance has a place among our street names, but it would seem that slaughter does too – how about Cut Throat Lane for a name? So here's a selection:

Cold Bath Road

Haywra Street

Penny Pot Lane

Cruet Fold

Barefoot Street

Water Skellgate

Raw Gap

Water Bag Bank

My Love Lane

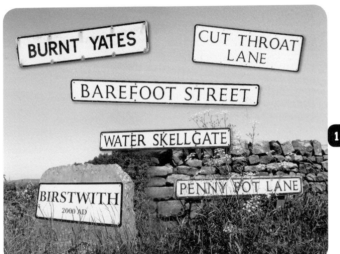

Suburbs of Harrogate

A fair number of Harrogate's suburbs can be described as affluent, with gracious old houses situated along tree-lined roads. Unusually, for the most part, these are to be found fairly close to the town's centre, where normally one would expect to find slums. Slums – in Harrogate!

Even the few suburbs which house residents on the most modest of incomes could not be thus described. Over the years, the town has gradually expanded and developed neighbourhoods for those who fall into the various middle classes. There are lots of these areas, with plenty of *des res* homes in them. There are few 'commercial and industrial' zones and the business sectors they cover are very light. The suburb of Central Harrogate is characterised by the huge green area of 'The Stray'.

And then there's:

Bilton: Within the boundary of the Royal Forest of Knaresborough.

Duchy: Roads named after dukedoms, except three – which are named after earldoms.

Harlow Hill: Roman coins have been found at Harlow Hill.

High Harrogate: Bronze axe heads found near St John's.

Hornbeam Park: Originally the home of ICI Fibres.

Jennyfields: The middle of the housing estate was once Corporation Farm.

Knox: Spruisty Packhorse Bridge over Oak Beck is Grade II listed.

Low Harrogate: Hub of most of the tourist activity.

New Park: There's been a hotel here since 1896.

Oatlands: Old railway tunnel leading to Harrogate's original station, abandoned in 1862.

Pannal: On 27 December 1304 King Edward I ordered weekly markets to be held here on Tuesdays.

Starbeck: The railway station dates from 1 September 1848.

Wheatlands: The historic Tewit Well stands on the edge of The Stray beside this suburb.

Woodlands: Harrogate Town Football Club is in this area.

Harrogate District

There's more to Harrogate than just the township – there's an entire administrative district, which was formed on 1 April 1974 under the Local Government Act of 1972. The Act merged various rural and urban districts, but in the process Harrogate lost four parishes, which then came under the administration of York. The following towns now come under the umbrella of Harrogate Borough Council:

Boroughbridge. This was the main coaching town between Edinburgh and London; it had twenty inns!

Knaresborough. Edward III's wife, Philippa of Hainault, loved Knaresborough Castle and spent many holidays there.

Masham. This has the largest market square in Yorkshire and two breweries.

Pateley Bridge. In the heart of Nidderdale: the start and finish of the Nidderdale Way walk is here.

Ripon. Ripon has honorary city status. Its first cathedral was built in AD 672, the present one in 1180.

There are also 150 villages and hamlets scattered around this largely rural area, as well as most of the Nidderdale Area of Outstanding Natural Beauty.

Demographics

These figures are for Harrogate and District:

Area: 504 square miles (133,060 hectares)

Total number of residents: 158,000

Spread of population: 70 per cent of the population live in the district's main towns

Ethnicity:
White: 98.4 per cent

Mixed: 0.7 per cent

Asian: 0.2 per cent

Black: 0.2 per cent

Chinese or other: 0.5 per cent

Life expectancy for babies born locally: seventy-six years for males; eighty (and a half) years for females.

Distance from Harrogate

	Km	Miles
Fortnum & Mason, London	336	209
Tower of London	341	212
Galeries Lafayette, Paris, France	777	483
Eiffel Tower, Paris, France	785	488
The Taj Mahal Hotel, Delhi, India	9,906	6,155
The Taj Mahal, Agra, India	10,120	6,288
Moss & Spy, Double Bay, NSW, Australia	6,917	10,507
Sydney Opera House, NSW, Australia	16,930	10,520
Bijan, Rodeo Drive, Beverley Hills, LA	8,506	5,287
Universal Studios, Hollywood, LA	8,527	5,302
Hermès, 691 Madison Ave, New York	5,598	3,479
Grand Central Station, New York	5,431	3,378
Wako, The Ginza, Tokyo	9,465	5,881
Senso-ji Temple, Tokyo	9,474	5,887
Peck, Via Spadari, Milan	1,606	998
The Last Supper, painting by da Vinci	1,605	997
Sun Tung Lok, Hong Kong	9,617	5,976
The Peak, Hong Kong	9,626	5,982
Cafè Florian, Venice	1,848	1,148
St Mark's Basilica, Venice	1,848	1,148

Get Your Bearings

Standing with your back to Betty's Café Tea Rooms' entrance:

Go downhill, to your left, for the Victorian Turkish Baths, Harrogate International Centre and the Royal Hall.
The Tourist Information Centre, the Royal Pump Room Museum and the Mercer Art Gallery are also nearby.

Turn right and cross the road ahead of you to get to The Stray – 200 acres of land enfolding the main urban 'old town'.

Turn right, following the windows around the corner, and go down the hill to reach the Montpellier Quarter. Just the place if you like exclusive shops, art and antiques.

Go straight across the road, and beyond the war memorial there are shops galore, on Cambridge Street to your left and James Street to your right.

MONTPELLIER QUARTER

Montpellier Parade

(from the hill from Bettys, towards the Crown Road)

No.1   Bettys   Café & Tearooms
No.2   Oxfam
No.4   Mum Bar Café   Bar Restaurant with Live

No.5   The Cheese   Restaurant
No.7   Le Jardin Café & Bistro   Bar & Restaurant
No.8   Carobbon Garden interiors   Home Interiors & Gifts
No.9   London Home   Oriental Rugs & Carpets
No.10   Carobbon Garden interiors   Home Interiors & Gifts
No.12   Beaumont   Ladies, Gents & Kids Fashion
No.14   Walker Galleries   Contemporary Art Gallery
No.14   Montpellier Pub   Traditional Family Run Pub
No.14   Anna Louise & Lavender Laurs   Complimentary Healthcare
No.17   La Place Studio   Ladies & Gents Hairdressers
No.18   Catwalk Café   Café & Tearoom
No.21   The Harrott Cashmere Company   Cashmere & Woollen Specialist
No.23   John Lewis of Hungerford   Kitchen Specialist
No.25   Trets   Ladies Fashion
No.25   Pets 2 Go   Designer Ceramic Café
No.27   Townhouse   Kitchen Specialist
No.28   Farah's   Confectioner
No.29   West Park Café   Café & Restaurant
No.30   The Bridal Collection   Bridal Wear & Accessories
No.31   Rinco   Ladies Designer Fashion
     Boutique
No.34   Trenate Antiquities   Antiquities

Royal Parade

At the bottom of Montpellier Hill near the Crown Hotel, towards the Valley Gardens.

No.1-2   Elaine Phillips Antiques   Antiques & Interior Design
No.3   Quantro   Contemporary Restaurant
No.4   Bespoke Eyewear by Jameline   Designer Frames & Sunglasses
No.5   Smithfly Galleries   18th, 19th, & 20th Century Fine
     Paintings
No.1A   Cupcakes by Charley   Coffee & Cupcakes
No.2   The Old Salt Tavern   Bar & Brasserie
No.3   The Treasures Bureau   Roxery Lakes
No.30   David Love Antiques   Antiques

Cold Bath Road

Off the roundabout at the bottom of Montpellier Hill.

The White Hoart Hotel   Accommodation & Restaurant &
     Traditional Tearooms
The Fat Badger   Bar & Restaurant

Crown Place

The little cobbled street adjacent to the Pump Rooms Museum.

No.1   The Crown Hotel   Accommodation & Restaurant
No.3   108 Gallery   Contemporary Art Gallery

Crescent Road

Adjacent to the Valley Gardens and the Pump Rooms Museum.

The Drum Bar
Other   Darroughs Olden Pub with
     Traditional Gas Lighting
     Lighting, Mirrors & Lampshades

Swan Road

Adjacent to the Valley Garden and opposite the Pump Rooms Museum.

Jeremy Wood   Kitchen Specialist

Montpellier Road

Adjacent to the Crown Hotel adjoining Montpellier Gardens.

Twinned Towns

The very earliest evidence of town twinning was centuries ago, in AD 836, between Paderborn, Germany, and Le Mans, France. Modern town twinning started in the 1920s, with 'sister' relationships beginning even earlier in the twentieth century. After the Second World War, these ideas grew to encourage both cultural and commercial links with other countries.

Harrogate

Harrogate has been twinned with the spa town of Luchon in South West France since 1952. Luchon is Stage 16 of the Tour de France cycle race, so Bradley Wiggins, the first Brit to win the coveted yellow jersey, knows the area well. I doubt he had time to look at the walls of the twelfth-century church of St Aventin and its wonderful 800-year-old murals, however.

Harrogate also has sister-city relationships with Wellington, New Zealand, and Harrogate, Tennessee.

St Aidan's Church of England High School, Harrogate, is twinned with Instituto Salmantino de Lenguas in Spain and Lycee Climatique d'Etat Jean Prévost in France.

Ripon

Ripon is twinned with Foix, France, a small city which is the capital of the Ariège departement. The Chateau de Foix, which dominates the whole area, was constructed around the year 1000.

Knaresborough

Knaresborough is twinned with the German town of Bebra in the Hersfeld-Rotenburg district in north-eastern Hesse. It was first mentioned in 786 as a donation to the nearby Benedictine abbey at Bad Hersfeld.

Namesakes

Harrogate, Tennessee, USA: Known as Harrogate since the 1800s, it became a city in 1993.

Harrogate, British Columbia, Canada: Lies beside the Columbia River, halfway between Yoho National Park and Kootenay National Park.

Harrogate, Queensland, Australia: Founded by the second Premier of South Australia in 1858, and named after the UK town.

Masham, Oklahoma, USA: Situated in Pawnee County, Masham's elevation is 961ft.

Ripon, California, USA: The first known humans here were the Laquisimne tribe.

Ripon, Wisconsin, USA: Birthplace of the Republican Party in 1854.

Ripon, Quebec, Canada: The original township was surveyed by an engineer born in Ripon, England.

Historical Timeline

Ripon Cathedral,
founded by
St Wilfred, was
dedicated

Building started
on Fountains
Abbey

Dr Michael Stanhope
found St John's Well,
also known as the
Sweet Spa

First human
settlement in
the Harrogate
District

Chenaresburg
(Knaresborough)
appears in the
Domesday Book

John of Gaunt
built a new
hunting lodge
in Bilton Park

The railway
reached
Harrogate

c. 4500 BC 672 1086 1134 1380 1631 1848

c. AD 72 700 1100 1156 *c.* 1596 1842

Bilton, now a
Harrogate suburb,
already existed

Jervaulx
Abbey
founded

The Royal
Pump Room
was erected

Romans
built a fort at
Boroughbridge

First
Knaresborough
Castle built

Sir William Slingsby
discovered spa
water at Tewit Well

Harrogate's
first public
library opened

The first council houses
were built in Stockwell
Avenue, Knaresborough; the
first in Harrogate were built
five years later

Tewit Well
was sealed

Harrogate
wins awards
including RHS
Discretionary
Award for the
Best Public Park

Harrogate
Theatre opened

The Royal Pump
Room became a
museum

1887   1900   1920   1953   1971   2009

1884   1897   1903   1946   1969   1982

Harrogate was
incorporated
(given a
mayor and
corporation)

The Kursaal
was built
and renamed
the Royal
Hall in 1918

The
Baths
closed

Eurovision Song Contest
held in Harrogate's
newly opened
Conference Centre
(Germany won)

Harrogate got
an electricity
supply

The Northern Horticultural Society founded; opened
the Harlow Carr Botanical Gardens in 1950; merged
with the Royal Horticultural Society in 2001

Freak Weather

1905: The Ripon Canal and the River Ure froze. People took advantage of this and got their ice skates out.

1933: 3ft (0.91m) of snow fell on Harrogate in three days.

1947: This was such a severe winter that nobody who experienced it could ever forget it. In Nidderdale, over 1,000 sheep were buried for a fortnight on the moors at Stean and Lofthouse.

1956: A prolonged drought in September resulted in a hosepipe ban in Ripon.

1962: On 12 February, a 100mph gale blew down 800 mature trees in Harrogate and left hundreds more in a dangerous condition. It also blew the Observatory's dome off and sent Knaresborough Town Hall's bell tower crashing through the roof.

1965: A combination of heavy rain and thawing snow resulted in severe floods in Pateley Bridge.

1968: Freak weather conditions on 2 July caused an inky darkness to descend on Harrogate at 10.45 a.m. Then came hailstones the size of golf balls…

1990: The highest temperature ever recorded in Harrogate was measured on 2 August, at over 91 degrees Fahrenheit.

1991, 1995, 2000, 2005 and 2007: Floods in Ripon.

Night Vision

1192: Late one cold January afternoon, people living in the area now described as Harrogate and District would have seen a sensational phenomenon occurring in the sky above them: an aurora borealis (or the Northern Lights).

This spectacular natural phenomenon was visible across the North of England, and as far away as Belgium, Western Germany and the present-day Czech Republic.

1938: Another aurora borealis was visible throughout the county on 25 and 26 January.

1949: And yet another, oddly enough also on 25 and 26 January.

1991: The Northern Lights were seen once again in Harrogate on 8 November.

2008: 8 August brought several reports of strange red lights moving slowly over Ripon and Masham. It happened again the following week.

According to UFO researchers, Yorkshire is the UK's top location for spotting UFOs, but sometimes things are not quite what they seem. In January 2009 two objects were spotted hovering in the sky above Bilton, but the mystery was solved three days later; they turned out to be Christmas lanterns. But sightings of bright orange lights in Harrogate in October 2011 and August 2012 certainly weren't lanterns – their departures were far too rapid.

No little green men have arrived so far – but when they do, they'll probably head straight for Betty's.

The Day the Earth Moved

At 9 p.m. on 3 January 2011, an earthquake struck the Harrogate district.

It had a magnitude of 3.6 and its epicentre was 5.5 miles north-west of Ripon, in the Kirkby Malzeard area.

Although Dr Aoife O'Mongain, of the British Geological Survey, said it 'only lasted for a couple of seconds', some locals thought it lasted longer than that. One of them said, 'The house shook for four or five seconds' and another thought it lasted three seconds. It caused part of the dry stone wall at the bottom of my garden to collapse.

Animals usually react to these things, and a student reported that his dogs started barking.

According to the British Geological Survey, it was the biggest earthquake in this part of North Yorkshire since 1780. That one measured 4.8 and occurred in Wensleydale, while a 3.1 tremor shook Skipton in 1900.

Literary Quotations

A character in Dr Tobias Smollett's novel *The Expedition of Humphry Clinker* says of Harrogate's spa water, 'I have drank it once and the first draught has cured me of all desire to repeat the medicine'.

We can understand why from this graphic description in another novel, *A Season at Harrogate*, by Mrs Barbara Hofland, published in 1812:

> 'Of rotten eggs, brimstone, and salts make a hash,
> And 'twill form something like this delectable mash
> Nothing else in this world I will wager a pasty.
> So good in effect, ever tasted so nasty.'

Eli Hargrove from Knaresborough gives another perspective on the town in his book *A Week at Harrogate*, which was published in 1814 – a perspective not so very different from today:

> 'Here a very great number of shops may be seen,
> All arrang'd, in a row, on the side of the green –
> Jewellers, milliners, tailors, and drapers,
> Perfumers, and druggists, and boot and shoe-makers.'

In *Henry V, Act II*, Shakespeare has the king saying, 'Now sits the wind fair, and we will aboard. My Lord of Cambridge, and my kind Lord of Masham, And you, my gentle knight, give me your thoughts.'

A Ballad

The Origin of Harrogate

A stranger stood upon the heath
As the sun was sinking down;
Before him rose the streets and towers
Of a fair and pleasant town:

An aged sire with locks of grey
Stood near that stranger man;
When to him turned the wondering one
And thus to speak began:

'Say, canst thou tell me, aged man,
What is the place I see?
Or why so fair a town was built,
'Midst such sterility.

For, unlike towns of ancient date,
It stands upon no rock;
No mighty castle's walls are seen,
The warriors' strength to mock.

It sleeps not in the sheltered vale,
Where oaks and wheat abound;
But proudly stands to brave the gale
In strength, with splendour crown'd.'

'The place thou seest,' the old man said,
'Is not unknown to fame;
Though young in years 'tis widely known,
And Harrogate its name.

The reason why it stands so high,
Exposed on every hand,
Is that health-giving fountains flow
From out the barren land.

Had they not been, thou ne'er hadst seen
Yon town before thee stand;
But wide had spread the forest dread
O'er all the savage land.

The equal hand of Providence,
That makes mankind its care,
Does blessings round to all dispense!
Yes, all receive a share.

To some the golden mine is given,
To some the corn and wine;
But water — peerless water!
Harrogate, is thine!'

Mr William Grainge of Harrogate

Famous for

These days, shopping!

But originally Harrogate shot to fame as a spa town, whose reputation attracted royalty from across Europe to try its various cures and sample its bracing air. They were swiftly followed by the great and the good, as well as the middle classes with delusions of grandeur.

In 1842 the Royal Pump Room had 3,778 visitors. By 1867 this had more than tripled to 11,626, and in 1925 it soared to almost 260,000. It's now a museum, but you can still see and smell the water from its sulphur well which flows 'on demand' from a tap outside the museum. Unfortunately, thanks to EU bureaucracy, tasting it is no longer permitted.

In addition to drinking the waters, some of the remedies on offer were:

Sulphur, carbonic acid, peat, sulphur foam or thermo-paraffin-wax baths

A couple of different douches

Massages

Harrogate's various spa treatments were reputed to cure all sorts of ailments. Among many others, these included:
Diseases affecting the joints or ligaments

Skin complaints

Heart disease

Constipation

Also Famous for

Betty's Café Tea Rooms. This most British of establishments was founded by a Swiss baker called Frederick Belmont in 1919. Unusually, given today's business climate, Betty's is still owned by the same family. They maintain the principles that guided Frederick when he set up the business, namely 'doing things beautifully' and taking good care of their customers.

How Stean Gorge. This spectacular limestone ravine is a Site of Special Scientific Interest and can be explored using paths or the Via Ferrata. Keep your eyes open for hidden treasure: Roman coins were found here in 1868.

The Stray. This is 200 acres of open grassland which belong to the people of Harrogate. This ownership was first formalised in 1778 and upheld by various Acts of Parliament since then, the latest enacted in 1985. It is vigorously protected by The Stray Defence Association, founded in 1933 to 'safeguard Harrogate's Stray against building and encroachment from all quarters' – which they successfully do.

Fountains Abbey: 'Fountains, where … so many drank of waters springing up to eternal life.' (William of Newburgh.) Founded in the 1130s by some disgruntled monks from St Mary's Abbey in York, Fountains became the largest and richest Cistercian abbey in the country. This World Heritage site contains the oldest surviving Cistercian watermill.

RHS Garden at Harlow Carr. This was originally part of a royal hunting ground. In 1950 the Northern Horticultural Society opened Harlow Carr Botanical Gardens, principally to trial plants suitable for growing in the North of England. In 2001 they merged with the Royal Horticultural Society. The original 10.5 hectares has expanded to 27.5 hectares and development of this lovely garden is ongoing.

The Devil's Arrows, Boroughbridge: There used to be at least four of these huge standing stones, according to a visitor in the 1530s, but only three remain, one of which is taller than Stonehenge's monoliths. They probably came from Plumpton Rocks, 16km (10 miles) away.

Infamous for

…Becoming a refuge for Agatha Christie when she went 'missing' in 1926.

Following a quarrel when her husband told her he wanted a divorce, this best-selling author promptly disappeared. Like a plot from one of her detective novels, the only clues were her abandoned car and a letter to her secretary saying she was going to Yorkshire.

She did indeed go to Yorkshire. Under an assumed name, she stayed at a hotel, now called The Old Swan, in the middle of Harrogate.

Despite the national hue and cry, the discreet staff and guests didn't let on that they had a celebrity in their midst – even though she had, of course, been recognised. However, after eleven days of this someone gave her away.

You can still dine in the hotel's Wedgwood Restaurant and imagine Agatha Christie sitting alone at a nearby table.

'Snorting Steeds'

'Snorting Steeds' was the *Harrogate Advertiser*'s description of the steam engines which brought the railway age to Harrogate.

* The first train reached Harrogate in July 1848, pulling into Brunswick station (near where Trinity Methodist church now stands). In 1859 a porter died here when he was crushed between the buffers of two wagons.

* The present Harrogate station opened in 1862, as the railway line was not allowed to cross The Stray. It was rebuilt between 1963 and 1965. The first stationmaster, Charles Matthews, ended up spending six months in hospital in 1866 when he tried to evict a number of militia men from the station and was beaten up by them.

* In 1900 a first-class season ticket from Harrogate to Leeds cost £15 per annum.

* Boroughbridge station opened in 1847; Ripon opened in 1848, and Masham in 1875. All closed in the 1960s.

* The first station in Knaresborough was Hay Park Lane. In July 1851 the permanent station was opened beyond the viaduct – which had collapsed just before it was completed and had to be rebuilt. A local astrologer was able to say, 'I told you so!'

* 3,000 people gathered at Ripon station (which, incidentally, was a mile outside town) to see Queen Victoria when her train stopped there for five minutes in September 1858.

* The Nidd Valley Railway operated from 1862 between Nidd Valley Junction near Killinghall and Pateley Bridge, closing in 1964.

* Nidd Valley Light Railway began as a 3ft gauge contractor's railway covering the 6 miles between Pateley Bridge and Lofthouse. Opened in September 1907, it closed to passengers in December 1929, closing completely in 1937.

Buried Treasure

In January 2007 a Viking treasure hoard, which had been stashed away in AD 927, was discovered in a field near Harrogate. The British Museum describes it as 'one of the most important finds of its type in Britain'.

Initially it was known as the Ballcock Hoard, because the finders thought they'd found something from a lavatory cistern. Then the name was changed to the Harrogate Hoard. It is now called the Vale of York Hoard, the name change being made to enable necessary funding to be obtained so that the collection could be purchased and put on display.

A beautifully engraved small bowl was packed with lots of coins, ornaments and ingots. These originated from such diverse places as Afghanistan, Iraq and Russia, as well as Ireland, Scandinavia and Europe.

In today's money it's worth over £1 million, but at the time it was buried – maybe two horses.

Sites of Special Scientific Interest

There are twenty-five sites of Special Scientific Interest in the area under Harrogate Council's control. Some of these are:

Birkham Wood, Knaresborough: two distinct types of woodland.

Bishop Monkton Ings: varied range of wetland habitats.

Burton Leonard Lime Quarry: nationally important grassland plants, including many rare species.

Cow Myers, near Galphay: extensive wetland plant communities.

East Nidderdale Moors: upland dry heath with blanket bog supporting bird populations of European importance.

Gouthwaite Reservoir, Nidderdale: reservoir of national importance for feeding ducks and waders.

Hackfall Wood, Grewelthorpe: ancient, largely undisturbed woodland.

Hay-a-Park, Knaresborough: important populations of wintering wildfowl and other wild birds.

Upper Nidderdale, Lofthouse: A geological SSSI centred on the underground course of the River Nidd and How Stean Gorge.

West Nidderdale: internationally important blanket bog and heather moorland supporting important breeding bird populations.

Nature's Playground

This 50-acre site is better known as Brimham Rocks. There's moorland and woodland to roam around, as well as terrific views across the Nidd valley. But it is best known for a remarkable variety of weird rock formations.

During the course of the last Ice Age, exposure to all sorts of weather conditions and water movement have produced rock shapes reminiscent of a dancing bear, an eagle and a blacksmith's anvil, as well as many other odd shapes.

The direction in which the water flowed can be clearly seen on some of the rocks. Just as an ebb tide can leave a ripple effect on the sand, so a similar impression can be seen on some of these Millstone Grit giants.

But the rocks arrived there long before the erosion started – around 430 to 380 million years ago, in fact. Grit and mud, washed down from massive mountains to the north, gradually compacted and hardened.

It used to be thought that the rocks had been carved by man. It's only during the past couple of centuries that geologists have informed us differently.

Plant Life

There are two cultivated flowers named after Harrogate:

The **Harrogate Rose** made its first appearance at the Northern Horticultural Society's Spring Flower Show in 2008. This yellow hybrid tea flowers from June to November.

Calamintha Harrogate is a mint-scented perennial. It has a mass of small blue flowers during summer and autumn and grows to about 12in high. Bees love it.

Wild plants of the region:

Thistle broomrape is found only in Yorkshire, mostly around Ripon and in the Leeds/Wetherby area. It is sometimes known as the Yorkshire broomrape. This plant is protected under Schedule 8 of the Wildlife and Countryside Act (1981).

Killarney fern only occurs in its immature form in Harrogate District and has been recorded at seven sites.

Dutch rush or rough horsetail is known in just one locality, in the Nidd Gorge.

Yellow star of Bethlehem is a local species which grows in woodland and on river banks.

Herb Paris is an indicator of ancient woodland.

The fern **Pillwort** and the liverwort **Violet crystalwort** (both rare plants, occurring naturally at one site each) are also found nearby.

Harrogate & District in Bloom

The Harrogate district won in eleven categories of the 2011 Yorkshire in Bloom competition (part of RHS Britain in Bloom) – the most wins in any one area since the awards began in 1964.

And the winners were:
Large Town/Small City (35-100k pop): Harrogate – gold award, and category winner.

Village: Spofforth – gold award, and joint category winner with Redbourne.

Urban Community: Starbeck – gold award, and category winner.

Town: Knaresborough – gold award, and category winner.

Large Town/Small City (12-35k pop): Ripon – silver gilt award, and category winner.

Business Premises: Betty's and Taylors of Harrogate – gold award, and joint category winner with Sheffield Forgemasters.

Country Houses, Estates, Parks and Gardens: Newby Hall and Gardens – gold award, and category winner.

Spring Floral Award: Winner, Starbeck.

Summer Floral Award: Winner, Harrogate.

Commercial Award: Winner, Betty's and Taylors of Harrogate.

Chairman's Award: Winner, Betty's and Taylors of Harrogate.

"Communities Growing Together"

Part of RHS Britain in Bloom

Wildlife

Three breeds of wild deer live in the Deer Park at Studley Royal: red, fallow and sika.

Eight species of bat can be found locally: whiskered, Brandt's, Daubenton's, natterer's, common pipistrelle, soprano pipistrelle, noctule and brown long-eared.

The **chestnut click beetle** is only found at two locations in Britain: one of them is a nature reserve near Harrogate.

The **square-spotted clay moth** is found in a highly significant cluster near Ripon.

Birdlife includes **merlin**, **buzzard**, **red kite**, **hen harriers**, **kestrels**, **wood warbler**, **marsh** and **willow tits**, **nightjar**, **lesser redpoll**, **tree pipit**, **long-eared owl**, **red grouse**, **golden plover**, and **pied flycatcher**.

Otters are present over much of the district, our watercourses providing important corridors for otter distribution.

Harrogate district has a healthy population of **great crested newts**, with about sixty breeding sites known, including a section of the Harrogate-Leeds railway line!

Our rivers are home to **depressed river mussel**, **fine-lined pea-mussel**, **white-clawed crayfish** and **ruffe** (a fish) – declining nationally, but spawning confirmed in the district.

High Batts hosts nine Red Data Book and thirteen nationally scarce species of fly.

Rebellious Harrogate

Modern Harrogate hosts few rebellions. Recently, the strongest it has seen have been an anti-fur demonstration and campaigns against Third World debt. A lone woman holding out against an army is in a different league altogether. That woman was Jane Ingilby, and the incident took place during the English Civil War.

Just outside Harrogate is Ripley Castle, home for seven centuries to the Ingilby family. The formidable Jane, according to the legend, fought alongside her brother, Sir William, at the Battle of Marston Moor. They returned to Ripley Castle when the Royalists were defeated – with Oliver Cromwell close behind.

Sir William hid in the priest hole when Cromwell pounded on the front door. But the forty-three-year-old Jane was not a woman to be trifled with, and she refused to let him in! Eventually he was allowed to spend the night in the castle – but he spent it looking down the barrel of Jane's pistol. She would give him shelter, but that was it; no searching the place to look for her beloved brother. The following morning, she sent Cromwell packing.

She probably inherited her rebellious nature from her father, who had close connections with the Gunpowder Plot conspirators.

Civil War bullet holes on the east wall of Ripley's church give testimony to just what a dangerous game Jane was playing. They were made when the Roundheads executed prisoners they had taken at the Battle of Marston Moor.

Walks

There are routes suitable for everyone. Here are just a few of the many available:

A circular walk around the edge of The Stray: 3 miles.

Start in Valley Gardens and walk 3 miles through woodland to RHS Harlow Carr.

Walk 7 miles along the Nidd Gorge, from Bilton to Knaresborough Castle.

The Harrogate Ringway, around the outskirts of the town, is 21 miles.

Even more challenging is the Harrogate Dalesway, which is 81 miles and can be joined in Valley Gardens.

The 53-mile Nidderdale Way begins and ends in Pateley Bridge, with stunning views along the way.

On the other hand, a walk around Fewston Reservoir is fairly easy, going for 3.7 miles.

How Stean Gorge offers a short walk – but not for the fainthearted!

From Boroughbridge you can walk into Roman history for 3.5 miles.

Masham Leaves Walk is 3 miles long; it follows a sculpture trail.

Nature Reserves

Birk Crag (1 mile south-west of Harrogate): roughly 27 hillside acres of mixed woodland.

Rosset (2 miles south-west of Harrogate town centre): small, but designated as a Site of Importance for Nature Conservation.

Hookstone Wood (2 miles south-east of Harrogate town centre): mixed woodland. Two ponds are included on the Special Invertebrate Interest Register.

Quarry Moor (1 mile south of Ripon): variety of wildlife and unique geology. Wheelchair friendly.

High Batts (3.7 miles north of Ripon): small private reserve. A varied habitat and easy walks.

Ripon Loop (0.75 miles north of Ripon): noted for its population of thistle broomrape.

Upper Dunsforth Carr (3 miles south of Boroughbridge): rare marshland insects, and over 100 species of moth.

Staveley (2.75 miles south-west of Boroughbridge): shallow lagoon. 230 plant species and 205 species of bird have been recorded.

Bishop Monkton Railway Cutting Nature Reserve (8 miles north of Harrogate): over 170 plant species have been logged.

Burton Leonard Lime Quarries (7 miles north of Harrogate): a rich diversity of flowering plants has encouraged about twenty different butterfly species.

Harrogate's Diamonds

In Dr Thomas Short's *History of Mineral Waters*, published in 1734 (and presumably referring to Bogs Field, in what is now Valley Gardens), he says:

'…about 200 yards south-east of the Bogg, when the ground is new plow'd, or harrow'd, and has a shower of rain, follow'd with a bright sunbeam, there are found beautiful, small, hard, transparent stones called diamonds.'

They weren't really diamonds, but crystals which had been produced through reaction of the mineral properties of the local spring water. Nonetheless, just like diamonds you could use these crystals to write your name on a piece of glass.

Some Facts about Harrogate & District

The population of Harrogate doubled between 1885 and 1900.

Mrs Gaskell's *The Life of Charlotte Bronte* refers to a trip that Branwell Bronte made to Harrogate with his mistress, Mrs Robinson. While there, Branwell's mistress suggested they should elope together, but he refused – despite 'the yearning love he still bore to the woman who had got so strong a hold upon him.'

Harrogate was in the West Riding of Yorkshire until 1 April 1974.

Work began on the Ripon Canal in 1767 and cost £16,400 (over £1 million in today's money). It is only 2.3 miles (3.7 km) long.

Andrew Carnegie, one of the most important philanthropists of his era, financed the building of the Central Library in Harrogate in 1906. However, he drew the line at donating further funds to build new council offices on land next to the library – so we've got some lovely gardens on the site instead.

The oldest sweetshop in England was established in Pateley Bridge in 1827.

There are two breweries in Masham: Theakston's and Black Sheep. Not bad for a village with fewer than 1,300 people in it!

In 1850 the well-preserved body of a Roman soldier was found in the peat on Grewelthorpe Moor.

The caves now known as Stump Cross Caverns were discovered in either 1858 or 1860 by William and Mark Newbould, miners who were searching for lead seams. Stump Cross originally marked the boundary between Bolton Priory and Fountains Abbey lands. More recently the caves have been designated a Site of Special Scientific Interest. In 1963 Geoff Workman, for research purposes, spent 105 days on his own in the caves – a world record.

A Druids' Temple

The Druids' Temple at Ilton (near Masham) is not of Druidic origin, nor is it a temple! It's not all that old either: it is probably best described as a glorious folly.

It was built around 1800 on the instructions of William Danby, the local landowner.

It lies north-west of Ilton on the Earl of Swinton's estate, and there is a parking area for public use.

The temple consists of an outer circle of trilithons interspersed with monoliths. Half a dozen more monoliths form an inner circle. There are also two 'altars'.

It is said that William Danby was willing to provide food to anyone who was prepared to live as a hermit within the temple for seven years, not communicating with anyone or even having a shave and a haircut now and again. At the end of his stint, the man would be given an annuity and become a gentleman. The story asserts that several men took up the challenge, but none managed the stipulated seven years. Not surprising, really, given Yorkshire's winters!

That's Entertainment!

There are six columns at the front of the Harrogate International Centre, which look out of place against its very modern design. They are, in fact, a nod to an earlier building which occupied the site: the Royal Spa Concert Room and Pleasure Grounds.

Designed by John Clarke of Leeds and built in 1835, this popular meeting place was fronted by iron gates. A few stone steps led to a portico with six soaring, fluted columns hinting at the elegance to be found inside. A contemporary visitor described the scene in the 100ft-long ballroom as having 'a good sprinkling of people of almost every sort ... scattered over the floor'. He described the ladies' dresses as varying from their day clothes through to full evening dress. Concerts were held there too and famous entertainers of the day, such as the multi-talented Arthur Lloyd, also entertained visitors when they weren't receiving their medicinal treatments.

In the 6 acres (2.4 hectares) of grounds outside stood the Cheltenham Pump Room, built in 1870, which dispensed the curative waters discovered on the site. It was so named because its water was thought to be similar to those of the rival spa town.

Further outside entertainment was provided by a boating lake and skating rink and the end of the season was particularly celebrated. On the last Saturday in September 1880, there was a grand masquerade, bicycle and skating carnival 'which will be brilliantly illuminated'. Also promised was 'a grand comic burlesque, Dr Tanner after his 40 days fast, upon the baby elephant, supported by all the comic characters, waiting for the signal to feed.'

Turner's Tour

The great artist J.M.W. Turner RA visited Yorkshire many times. He was twenty-two when he first travelled to the North, in 1775, and he returned here throughout his life, visiting and painting or sketching in over seventy locations. Eleven pieces of art were composed in the Harrogate district:

Boroughbridge and **Ellenthorpe Hall**: he made four sketches of the bridge. He then walked along the river, where he drew a couple which included part of the medieval hall (which has now disappeared).

Cowthorpe: he did three studies of the 1,800-year-old Cowthorpe oak. It is no longer there, but the church in the background still is.

Dob Park Lodge, Washburn Valley: his watercolour painting is focused on a dead tree trunk, with the ruined towers in the background.

Fountains Abbey: he painted two watercolours, an external one of the dormitory and transept and another of the interior.

Hackfall: a famous wild garden in Turner's time. He did numerous sketches, two of which he later used to produce watercolour paintings.

Knaresborough Castle: he visited twice, making numerous sketches, and later developed watercolour paintings from them.

Masham Market Place: here he sketched riverside views near the bridge, and also a view of the town from the bridge.

Newby Hall: Turner made detailed sketches of the house and grounds when he visited in 1816.

Plumpton Rocks: the First Earl of Harewood commissioned two oil paintings, which Turner finished following his first visit to Yorkshire.

Ripon Cathedral and **Bell Banks** (Sharow): Turner visited Ripon twice, doing sketches of the old Ure Bridge and both internal and external views of the minster (as it was then).

Spofforth Castle: he also visited this location twice, making a watercolour from his sketched material.

Parks and Open Spaces

The Stray is mentioned elsewhere. There's also Valley Gardens, a 17-acre English Heritage Grade II listed garden.

In that part of Valley Gardens known as Bogs Field, more mineral springs surface than anywhere else in the world, including thirty-six of Harrogate's eighty-eight mineral wells – no two of them are alike. It is protected by an Act of Parliament and has decorated well heads, put there in the 1920s. About a decade before that, Alderman Binns was so determined that the park's boundary should be extended that he rolled his sleeves up and knocked down the dividing wall under cover of darkness! The park's first Superintendent, a Mr Chipchase, was appointed in 1887.

Killinghall Moor Country Park is a 25-acre conservation area in the Oakdale area of Harrogate which also has four senior and two junior football pitches. In 2004 the Football Association awarded the National Groundsman of the Year Award to the site's manager.

And in the district:

Spa Gardens and Spa Park, Ripon. The band of the 1st Battalion, the West Yorkshire Regiment, were the first to play on the bandstand when it opened in June 1902.

The Recreation Ground, Pateley Bridge. This area is also home to Bewerley Park, home to both North Yorkshire Council's Outdoor Education Centre and, each September, the wonderful Nidderdale Show (also known as the Nidderdale Rant at one time).

Jacob Smith Park, Conyngham Hall and Bebra Gardens, Knaresborough. Jacob Smith Park was originally part of the land belonging to Scriven Hall, the seat of the Slingsby family.

Boroughbridge tops the lot by having two national parks on its doorstep – the North York Moors and the Yorkshire Dales.

Businesses

A. Fattorini
In 1831, Antonio Fattorini moved to Harrogate and opened a jeweller's shop on Parliament Street. It is today directed by the great, great grandsons of the founder.

Farrah's of Harrogate
Founded by John Farrah in 1840, their Harrogate Toffee was originally made to dispel the awful taste that Harrogate's sulphur water left in the mouth. Nobody drinks the water now, but they still eat the toffee.

Fodder
Britain's first charitable food hall, with all profits re-invested to benefit the rural community. Located at the Great Yorkshire Showground in Harrogate, it stocks local food and produce.

Harrogate Advertiser
Founded in 1847. Its editor, Robert Ackrill, bought the paper from its owner and later bought out the competition too. Family owned until 1983, it was sold to United Newspapers and is now owned by Johnston Publishing Ltd.

Harrogate International Centre
One of the country's top venues for exhibitions, conferences, trade fairs, public shows, product launches, banquets and entertainments is owned by Harrogate Borough Council.

Harrogate Spring Water Ltd
Founded in 2002, their bottled water is sourced from water-bearing rocks near the centre of town. A step back in history!

Taylors of Harrogate
Founded in 1886 by Charles Taylor. He supplied tea designed to suit different types of water. They still make a Yorkshire Tea for Hard Water blend, especially composed to counteract the effect of hard water on your cuppa.

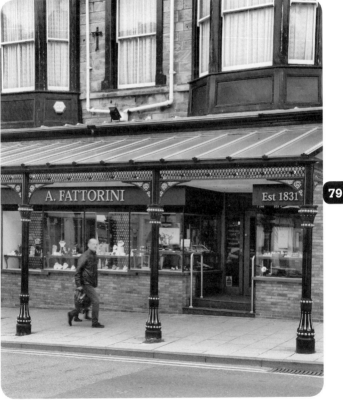

Architecture – Old and New

In 1664 there were just fifty-seven houses in Harrogate, two of which took in guests. As the town's reputation began to grow, so did the need for proper hotels. The first was the **Queen's Head** (where the Cedar Court Hotel now stands), possibly dating from as early as 1660 (although the present building only dates from 1855 and was enlarged in 1861).

As well as hotels, grand houses appeared – such as **Wedderburn House**, built in 1786 for Alexander Wedderburn MP, who was Lord Chancellor from 1793 to 1801.

And there was a need for entertainment after taking one's cure for the day. The **Promenade Room**, completed in 1806, is Harrogate's oldest spa building. It became a theatre for a while; it then had a spell as the Town Hall and later as council offices. Finally, in 1991, it was restored. It is now the Mercer Art Gallery.

And we still construct innovative buildings:

Harrogate has its very own pyramid. This office block in Hornbeam Park is over 130ft (40m) high and is made of stainless steel and glass.

Rivers

There are ten rivers running through Harrogate District:

The **Nidd** winds its way through Harrogate, Pateley Bridge and Knaresborough.

The **Crimple** flows west to east, 3.5 miles south of Harrogate past Beckwithshaw and Pannal.

Ripon has two rivers, the **Skell** and the **Laver**.

Boroughbridge has the **Ure** and the **Tutt.**

The **Ure** also flows through Masham, as does the **Burn.**

The **River Washburn** lies within the Nidderdale Area of Outstanding Natural Beauty.

Short stretches of the **Wharfe** and the **Ouse** run along the south-west and north-east borders of the district respectively.

Harrogate & District Personalities

Jim Carter: Harrogate born and educated actor; has appeared in numerous film and television productions including *Downton Abbey* (as Mr Carson).

Louisa Kruckenberg: this talented amateur photographer was born in Grewelthorpe; she died in 1958.

Squadron Leader James Harry 'Ginger' Lacey DFM and Bar: one of the top-scoring RAF fighter pilots of the Second World War. He attended King James Grammar School, in Knaresborough.

Sir Edward Hulton: founded the Hulton Press in 1937; published *Farmers' Weekly*, *Eagle*, *Girl*, *Picture Post*, *Lilliput* and *Leader Magazine*.

Samson Fox: mayor from 1890 to 1892. Helped to set up the town's fire service, supplied public street lighting and was a major force in getting the Royal Hall built to such a high standard.

Frederick Bower: A Ripon botanist and one of the foremost plant morphologists of his time; he published a three-volume work entitled *The Ferns*.

Betty Lupton, or **Old Betty**: a volunteer water server, elected Queen of the Wells each May for many years before her death in 1843. This tradition didn't survive for much longer.

Isabella Bird: was a middle-aged Victorian lady from Boroughbridge who decided to expand her horizons. She visited the Hawaiian Islands, the Rockies, Japan, Persia, Malaya, Kashmir, Tibet, China and Korea.

William Powell Frith: born in Aldfield in 1819; a significant painter of the social scene.

William Grainge: born in Kirkby Malzeard in 1818; wrote many history and topography books.

Blind Jack Metcalf: blind from childhood, this Knaresborough man built 180 miles (289km) of roads in the eighteenth century.

Mary Ward: born into a Roman Catholic family of landed gentry at Mulwith Manor near Boroughbridge, Mary founded an international community of nuns and was determined to educate women – not the 'done thing' in the early seventeenth century. She is now on the path to being made a saint.

'**Mother Shipton**': a medieval mystic who is said to have been born in a cave near Knaresborough in around 1488. She is reputed to have foretold various events and inventions.

St Robert: a twelfth-century hermit, whose cave home can be found near the River Nidd at Knaresborough.

Ghosts

Researchers have identified a 221-square-mile area between Harrogate, York and Leeds as the second most haunted place in Britain. It was also named as the country's top location for seeing UFOs.

Harrogate Theatre is said to be haunted by a friendly ghost called Alice, who fell to her death from the balcony.

Harrogate's **Ashville College** is apparently haunted by a former teacher named Mr Horsley.

Ripley Castle seems to have several ghosts, including a nun who knocks before entering a room.

Spofforth Castle has half a ghost: the top part of a bluish-white female briefly appears on the tower before throwing herself off.

Knaresborough's **Mother Shipton** returned to her cave home 500 years after her death to show herself to some tour guides.

Fountains Abbey's ghosts are heard but not seen – their chants drifting through the wonderful twelfth-century ruins.

Marston Moor is the site of a major Civil War battle where over 4,000 died. Men dressed in seventeenth-century clothing have been seen on a nearby road; they vanish shortly afterwards.

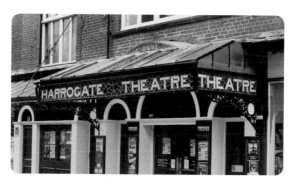

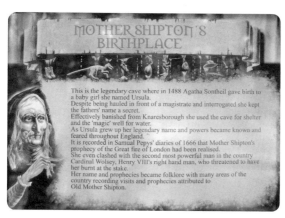

MOTHER SHIPTON'S BIRTHPLACE

This is the legendary cave where in 1488 Agatha Sontheil gave birth to a baby girl she named Ursula.

Despite being hauled in front of a magistrate and interrogated she kept the fathers' name a secret.

Effectively banished from Knaresborough she used the cave for shelter and the 'magic' well for water.

As Ursula grew up her legendary name and powers became known and feared throughout England.

It is recorded in Samual Pepys' diaries of 1666 that Mother Shipton's prophecy of the Great fire of London had been realised.

She even clashed with the second most powerful man in the country Cardinal Wolsey, Henry VIII's right hand man, who threatened to have her burnt at the stake.

Her name and prophecies became folklore with many areas of the country recording visits and prophecies attributed to Old Mother Shipton.

Harrogate in the Wars

Five Harrogate and District men have been awarded the Victoria Cross.

Four months after the Indian Mutiny began, **Sergeant Robert Grant** of the 1st Battalion, 5th Regiment of Foot saved a private's life.

In 1915 **Private Charles Hull** was also in India when he rescued an officer from certain death at the hands of tribesmen.

Temporary 2nd Lieutenant Donald Simpson Bell died in the Battle of the Somme in 1916, five days after knocking out an enemy machine-gun post.

Captain Archie White twice showed most conspicuous bravery at Stuff Redoubt in 1916.

Corporal Bryan Budd twice showed conspicuous gallantry, saving the lives of many of his colleagues in Afghanistan in 2006.

Stonefall Cemetery is the final resting place for servicemen from various countries:

Twenty-three First World War servicemen are buried or commemorated there.

Of the 988 Second World War servicemen buried there, nearly all are airmen.

Harrogate was bombed once – by a German Junkers 88. On 12 September 1940 it dropped three bombs on and near the Majestic Hotel, thinking the Air Ministry was using it as a headquarters. Fifteen people were injured, one of whom later died.

HARROGATE BORN RECIPIENTS

THIS PLAQUE IS DEDICATED TO THE MEMORY OF THE MEN
WHOSE SERVICE TO THEIR COUNTRY
EARNED THEM THE HIGHEST MILITARY HONOUR

THE VICTORIA CROSS

REMEMBER

T/2ND LIEUTENANT DONALD S. BELL VC
9TH BATT. THE YORKSHIRE REGIMENT
BORN 3RD DECEMBER 1890
AWARDED THE CROSS 5TH JULY 1916 SOMME FRANCE
KILLED IN ACTION 11TH JULY 1916

PRIVATE CHARLES HULL VC CROIX DE GUERRE
21ST LANCERS
BORN 24TH JULY 1890
AWARDED THE CROSS 5TH SEPTEMBER 1915 NORTH WEST FRONTIER INDIA
DIED AT LEEDS 15TH FEBRUARY 1920

SERGEANT ROBERT GRANT VC
1ST BATT. 5TH REGIMENT
BORN HARROGATE 1837
AWARDED THE CROSS 24TH SEPTEMBER 1857 ALUMBAGH INDIA
DIED IN LONDON 7TH MARCH 1857

PER ARDUA AD ASTRA

A Hidden Gem

It's easy to miss the sign for Plumpton Rocks, along the Harrogate/Wetherby road. It is well worth keeping an eye open for it, however, as it will lead you to 30 lovely acres of Grade II listed landscape garden.

The original manor was mentioned in the Domesday survey and was held by the de Plompton family. It continued in the same family's ownership from then until the mid-eighteenth century, when Robert de Plompton died leaving no male heirs.

A manor house is shown on Saxton's Map of 1577 and a 1587 map of the estate shows this surrounded by 'Plompton Parke'. The latter also shows the lake which had been formed by damming a beck which runs below the rocky outcrop of Millstone Grit and into the Crimple.

Both J.M.W. Turner and Thomas Girtin have painted the lake.

In 1755 Daniel Lascelles bought the estate with the intention of restoring the ruined manor house. Instead, he built the present Plompton Hall (which had originally been part of the manor's stable block).

It is open at weekends from 11 a.m. to 6 p.m between March and October.

Local Food and Drink

Ripon Spice Cake: depending which source you choose, this traditional loaf cake is described both as 'lightly spiced with mace and allspice' or 'a sweet, aromatic and heavily spiced loaf'.

Old Peculiar Cake: a fruit cake made with Theakston's Old Peculiar Ale (on sale at Betty's Café Tea Rooms).

Farrah's Original Harrogate Toffee: originally made, as mentioned earlier, to help remove the foul taste of Harrogate's sulphur water.

Ribston Pippin: this apple gets its name from Ribston Hall, Little Ribston, where it was first grown in the eighteenth century.

Yorkshire Tea: made by Taylors of Harrogate.

Harrogate Spring Water has a nice creamy flavour – much nicer than the water offered to cure all sorts of ailments when Harrogate was a popular spa.

Harrogate Nights: a cocktail made with vodka, peach schnapps, Malibu, fresh orange juice, fresh pineapple juice and fresh cranberry juice.

Masham Ale: Theakston's strongest beer is brewed in late November.

Riggwelter Ale: produced by the Black Sheep Brewery; according to local Dales-speak, a sheep is 'rigwelted' when it has rolled onto its back and can't get back up.

The Knights Templar

A Knights Templar preceptory was founded at Little Ribston, 7 miles east of Harrogate, in 1217, and seems to have originated from a gift of land by Robert de Ros.

This included a manor, vill and mill at Ribston, together with the advowson of the church at Walshford and the vill of Hunsingore, all inherited from Ros' mother, Rose Trussebut.

At some time before 1240 his maternal aunts, Hilary and Agatha, granted them various woods near the preceptory. At its height Ribston comprised more than 900 acres of arable land, 30 acres of meadow and four watermills.

The Templars also acquired further lands, mills and manors at Wetherby, Sicklinghall, Cowthorpe and Cattal – all local to Ribston – plus Ilkley, much further away.

All that remains of the Ribston Preceptory is the chapel, which now has the seventeenth-century Ribston Hall tacked onto one of its walls.

Harrogate in Days Gone By: The Stray

Harrogate in Days Gone By: Royal Baths

Royal Visits

Harrogate has attracted numerous royal visitors over the centuries, but the present royal family has made many visits to the town in the more recent past too:

The **Princess Royal** visited in 1972, 1981 and, most recently, in 2010, when she inspected a military graduation parade at the Army Foundation College.

Prince Andrew visited the college in 2011.

On 22 January 2008, the **Prince of Wales** officially re-opened the Royal Hall, having already visited twice to show his ongoing support and commitment as its patron.

Since moving permanently to its present site in Harrogate, The Great Yorkshire Show's royal visitors have been:

Princess Anne, 1994
Princess Alexandra, 1999
Prince Charles, 2000
The Duke and Duchess of York, 2002
The Duke of York, 2006
The Queen and the Duke of Edinburgh, 2008
The Prince of Wales and the Duchess of Cornwall, 2011

And finally …

In May 2010, Prince Harry dropped into the Banyan Bar on John Street for a burger and a pint of beer. A bodyguard asked a member of staff if he thought they'd have any problem with paparazzi. He replied, 'Not really … It's Harrogate!'

Listed Buildings

Harrogate District has just over 2,000 'listed buildings', sixty-eight of which are in Harrogate itself. The list includes sixteen churches, six hotels and three bridges, a viaduct and a cinema.

Some of Harrogate's listed buildings are:

Tewit Well: the earliest of the Harrogate chalybeate springs.

St John's Well: built in around 1842 on the site of an earlier well head, built in around 1786.

Magnesia Well Building in Valley Gardens: built in around 1858 in the Gothic style.

Royal Baths: built in 1894-97 by Baggerley Bristow. The original Harrogate coat of arms is still above the imposing entrance.

Mill Lane Boundary Stone: dated 1767, this square column is about 2ft tall and marks a boundary of the ancient forest of Knaresborough.

Stone Pillar (near south-east corner of West Park). Erected in 1778 and inscribed 'Boundary of the Leeds and Ripon Turnpike roads'.

Royal Pump Room Museum: built in 1842, on the site of sulphur springs described by Edmund Deane in 1626.

And among many others in the district:

Town Hall, Ripon

House in the Rock, Knaresborough

Masham Bridge

Aldborough Manor, Boroughbridge

No. 39 High Street (the oldest sweet shop in England)

Pateley Bridge

Harrogate in Days Gone By:
A View of Valley Gardens

Battlefields

Battle of Myton, 20 September 1319

This battle took place only partly in Harrogate District, being fought at the confluence of the Ure and Swale, near Boroughbridge. The Scots intended capturing Queen Isabella, then in York. They failed and started to return north. The Archbishop of York raised an army of 10,000 untrained men and chased the Scots, but his force was ambushed and slaughtered.

Battle of Boroughbridge, 16 March 1322

Thomas, Earl of Lancaster tried to overthrow Edward II. Having lost the fight at Burton-on-Trent six days earlier, Thomas decided to take refuge in Northumberland. He reached Boroughbridge, only to encounter Sir Andreas de Harcla with a 4,000-strong army. The rebels were beaten, and Thomas was captured and executed. The modern town covers part of the battlefield, but because it was a fight across the river it can still be envisaged.

Battle of Marston Moor, 2 July 1644

This Civil War encounter between 18,000 Royalists and 28,000 Roundheads started at 7 p.m. and just two hours later the Parliamentarians had won the battle. About 4,000 Royalists were killed. It is thought to be the largest battle fought on English soil.

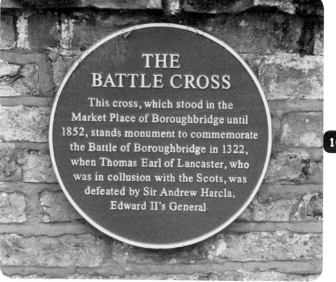

THE
BATTLE CROSS

This cross, which stood in the
Market Place of Boroughbridge until
1852, stands monument to commemorate
the Battle of Boroughbridge in 1322,
when Thomas Earl of Lancaster, who
was in collusion with the Scots, was
defeated by Sir Andrew Harcla,
Edward II's General.

Castles

Knaresborough Castle, Knaresborough: owned by a succession of kings, it now belongs to Queen Elizabeth II. It's in a perfect defensive position, high on a cliff above the River Nidd. Thomas Becket's murderers took refuge here.

Ripley Castle, Ripley: built in the fifteenth century, and owned by the Ingleby family since then. There's a medieval gatehouse; the tower is home to the Knight's Room and a priests' hole. There are also large formal walled gardens, begun in 1817.

Spofforth Castle, Spofforth: this fortified manor house was the original English home of the Percy family. Now a ruin, it was first built in the eleventh century; a stone hall house was added two centuries later, with the first-floor hall being modernised in the fifteenth century.

Allerton Castle, near Knaresborough: almost modern, as castles go! Originally known as 'Allerton Park', this Grade I listed nineteenth-century Victorian house was rebuilt by George Martin in 1843-53.

John O'Gaunt's Castle, Beckwithshaw: this was really a fortified royal hunting lodge in what was then part of Knaresborough Forest. Legend has it that Cromwell's cannon rendered it a ruin; bits of the wall remain.

Mowbray Castle, Kirkby Malzeard: in the heart of Nidderdale, this motte-and-bailey castle was first mentioned in 1131. Less than fifty years later, it was demolished, so that only an earthwork remains now.

Rougemont Castle, Kirkby Overblow: remains of defensive ditches and either a large outer enclosure or a bailey. It has also been suggested that these are, in fact, the remains of a fortified manor house.

Howe Hill Castle, near North Deighton: a motte with a mound surviving to a height of 20m; there may also have been a bailey.

Harrogate's Russian Duchess

H.I. and R.H. Grand Duchess George of Russia was loved by Harrogate people and every injured First World War soldier she met here. But what was she doing in Yorkshire in the first place?

In 1910 doctors said her children needed a complete change of air and recommended Harrogate. The Grand Duchess and her two daughters returned in July 1914 for a three-week visit – and became stranded here when war broke out. To make herself useful, she trained as a Red Cross nurse and then opened several hospitals, which she visited daily to talk to and care for the wounded. During her visits she often picked up lice from the patients, but shrugged it off as part of the job.

When looking for suitable premises to turn into hospitals, she found a convalescent home called Heatherdene. She had an operating theatre installed and provided a lot of new beds and equipment. Her little hospital has long since disappeared, but the site still exists and is now part of Harrogate District Hospital.

During the course of the war, more than 1,200 casualties passed through her hospitals, 127 of whom were local men. She spent her last Christmas with 'her' soldiers in 1918 and returned to Harrogate again on 27 March 1919 'for the sad business of closing my beloved hospitals.'

Many patients showed their gratitude and affection for her by giving her birthday and Christmas presents; she kept every one and described them as being 'among my most treasured possessions'. Some years later, a visitor to her apartment in Rome was shown into a room which the Duchess described as 'a spot that is forever England'. The walls were covered with framed photographs of her Harrogate soldiers, nurses and hospitals.

She died in Greece on 14 December 1940, at the age of sixty-four.

Film Locations

Escape from the Dark (1976)
Alastair Sim played Lord Harrogate in this film about the rescue of pit ponies. It included scenes shot at Ripley Castle.

Agatha (1979)
Vanessa Redgrave played the famous writer, with Timothy Dalton as her husband, in this late 1970s film about Christie's famous eleven-day disappearance. Scenes were shot at the Old Swan Hotel (where the real Agatha stayed), the Royal Baths Assembly Rooms, and surrounding streets in Harrogate.

Chariots of Fire (1981)
This classic, which won four Oscars (for costume design, music, best picture and best screenplay) and was nominated for another three (best actor for Ian Holm's performance, as well as another two nods for the director and the editor), included scenes shot at Crown Place, Crescent Gardens, Harrogate.

The Final Conflict (or Omen III) (1981)
Sam Neil played the lead in this horror, filmed at Fountains Abbey.

Wetherby (1985)
Vanessa Redgrave, Judi Dench and Ian Holm appeared in this film, which included scenes shot in and around Knaresborough and at Harrogate Grammar School.

The Secret Garden (1993)
Maggie Smith visited Fountains Hall and Allerton Park, Harrogate, to film this version of the classic children's story.

Wide-Eyed and Legless (1993)
This made-for-television film starring Julie Walters, Jim Broadbent and Thora Hird was filmed in Harrogate and surrounding area, and at Brimham Rocks.

Frankenstein (1994)
This version, starring Robert de Niro, Kenneth Branagh and Helena Bonham Carter, was filmed at Ripley Castle and in the village. Exactly ten years before, another version of the same story was filmed at the castle and on Rudding Park Estate.

Television Locations

The Duchess of Duke Street (1976)
Television series loosely based on the life of 'the Duchess of Jermyn Street', Rosa Lewis, the 'Queen of Cooks'. She worked for employers including Lady Randolph Churchill, the mother of Winston Churchill, and was rumoured to be one of Edward VII's mistresses. Scenes from this series were filmed at Ripley Castle.

A Woman of Substance (1984)
13.8 million people watched Deborah Kerr and Jenny Seagrove in this version of the classic novel, a record at the time. Scenes were filmed at Brimham Rocks.

Beiderbecke Affair (1985)
Forest Lane level crossing in Starbeck was used for a scene in this YTV production because there were no level crossings in Leeds.

The Adventures of Sherlock Holmes (1984-94)
The Sign of the Four was filmed at Allerton Park, Harrogate.

The New Statesman (1987-92)
Starbeck featured in an episode of this Yorkshire Television sitcom starring Rik Mayall.

God on the Rocks (1990)
Minnie Driver and Sinead Cusack appeared in this Harrogate-shot feature which also featured a cameo appearance by silent-film star Florence Hunter, aka 'Baby Twinkles'.

Darling Buds of May (1991-93)
This show launched Oscar-winning actress Catherine Zeta-Jones to fame. It used the terrace at Yorkshire Winery, Glasshouses, near Pateley Bridge.

The Mixer (1992)
Actress Rula Lenska, born Countess Roza-Marie Leopoldnya Lubienska, starred in two episodes of this good-natured 1930s-set series about a man and his butler who steal back stolen property. Scenes for *The Mixer* were shot in Harrogate town centre.

Ain't Misbehavin' (1994-95)

This sitcom, by the writer of *Last of the Summer Wine* and *Keeping up Appearances*, was filmed in Harrogate town centre and at Ripley Castle.

Mansfield Park (2007)

Child-star-turned-actress Billie Piper played Miss Fanny Price in ITV's adaptation of Jane Austen's novel of the same name. The film was shot almost entirely on location at Newby Hall. In an interview with the *Yorkshire Post*, the executive producer revealed that the main problems during filming were 'the wrong kind of sheep, modern hay stacking, non-period vehicles creeping into shot and planes circling overhead'.

Emmerdale (ongoing)

Soap opera filmed at Rudding Holiday Park and in and around Harrogate.

Harrogate in Days Gone By:
The Bandstand in Valley Gardens

Jubilee Trees

To celebrate Queen Elizabeth II's Diamond Jubilee, The Woodland Trust has invited people to plant trees. They discovered that something similar happened to celebrate King George VI's coronation. Harrogate doesn't appear in the records, but other towns and villages in the district do.

Ripon: Seventeen trees were planted on what was then an open space known as High Clough, and along Mallorie Park Drive; two oaks were planted at Hollin Hall. In addition, two children from each class in Ripon's schools, together with some of their friends, planted a total of 13,000 daffodil bulbs during the course of that coronation year. They also planted yellow crocuses in the shape of a crown with the letters GR incorporated in the design.

Pateley Bridge: Twenty trees were planted in the Recreation Ground by children from Bewerley Church of England School and Bishopside Council School.

Ripley: An avenue of twenty-six trees was planted at the southern end of the village.

Bishop Monkton: A red oak was planted in the centre of the village.

South Stainley: Eighteen schoolchildren planted a tree each along the Harrogate-Ripon road.

Things to do in Harrogate & District

Eat at:
Weeton's, overlooking The Stray, for breakfast.

Any one of over a dozen restaurants on Cheltenham Crescent for lunch or dinner.

Sightsee at:
RHS Harlow Carr for a stroll through a garden with stream and woodland planting.

Ripley Castle: look for the Roundheads' bullet holes in the church wall.

The Roman site at Aldborough to see mosaics and a section of the original town wall.

Masham Sheep Fair in September – well worth a visit.

Shop at:
Montpellier Quarter for antiques and chic clothes.

Parliament Street, James Street or Cambridge Street for more affordable shopping.

The many antique shops in Pateley Bridge.

Be entertained at:
Lightwater Valley, near Ripon.

Harrogate Theatre or the Royal Hall for a show.

Half a dozen different nightclubs.

Harrogate in Days Gone By: Prospect Place

Picture Credits

Page:

57. Great crested newts' breeding area beside the Harrogate-Leeds railway (Picture: Fallen Tree Originals)

59. Oliver Cromwell (1599-1658) at the Battle of Marston Moor, 2 July 1644 (Artist unknown, possibly Ernest Crofts. Picture: Wikimedia Commons)

Ripley Castle (Picture: Dposte46)

61. Slingsby Walk, The Stray (Picture: Fallen Tree Originals)

63. Thistle Broomrape, *Orobanche reticulata* (Picture: Nasko)

65. Uncut industrial-grade diamond (Picture: Dave Fischer)

67. Andrew Carnegie with his wife Louise Whitfield Carnegie, sister-in-law Estelle (Stella) Whitfield, and daughter Margaret (Picture: Library of Congress, LC-USZ62-79095)

69. Druids' Temple at Ilton (Picture: Fallen Tree Originals)

71. The six columns, steps and lions which used to stand at the entrance to the Royal Spa Concert Room. They are now to be found in the wooded area at RHS Harlow Carr (Picture: Fallen Tree Originals)

73. These decaying walls are the remains of Dob Park Lodge, a once-proud building which is falling apart at the seams. It is perched on high ground in the Yorkshire Dales in a spot which commands a fine view of the Washburn Valley's rolling landscape. The original photo is online in full resolution in this set of images (Picture: TJ Blackwell)

75. Newby Hall (Picture: Grahamec)

77. Spa Gardens, Ripon. These gates were presented to the City of Ripon on behalf of the Royal Engineers by General Sir Nevil Brownjohn on 27 July 1957 (Picture: David Rogers)

Devils' Arrows, Boroughbridge (Picture: Me677)

79. A. Fattorini, jewellers (Picture: Fallen Tree Originals)

81. Glass pyramid (Picture: Fallen Tree Originals)

Fountains Abbey (Picture: Johnteslade)

83. Washburn River at Blubberhouses (Picture: Fallen Tree Originals)

River Ure from the south bank of the river looking towards Ure Bank Terrace (Ripon) (Picture: David Rogers)

River Nidd weir at Birstwith (Picture: Fallen Tree Originals)

85. Frederick Orpen Bower, English botanist

87. Blind Jack of Knaresborough (Picture: THP)

89. Harrogate Theatre (Picture: Fallen Tree Originals)

Spofforth Castle (Picture: Immanuel Giel)

Information board at the entrance of Mother Shipton's cave in Knaresborough (Picture: Chris)

91. Memorial plaque for Harrogate's VC recipients (Picture: Fallen Tree Originals)

RAF (and other Commonwealth air forces) motto carved into a shelter in Stonefall cemetery (Picture: Redvers at en.wikipedia)

93. The sandstone features known as Plumpton Rocks in North Yorkshire have been admired by people wishing to capture their beauty since the sixteenth century – a map from 1587 shows the spot to be almost unchanged when compared to its current appearance. Today, it's mostly photographers like me and the chap depicted here who come to document its looks - but the rocks also appear in historical paintings by the likes of Thomas Girtin and J.M.W Turner (Picture: TJ Blackwell)

95. A Ribston Pippin apple on the tree (Picture: MarkusHagenlocher)

97. Knights Templar chapel attached to the Georgian Ribston Hall (Picture: Diane Holloway)

Looking over the River Nidd at the front of Ribston Hall (Picture: Thedavegray)

99. The Stray in 1900 (Picture: Library of Congress, LC-DIG-ppmsc-08421)

101. Royal Baths in 1900 (Picture: Library of Congress, LC-DIG-ppmsc-08422)

103. A long tradition of visits: The Queen in Australia with Prince Philip in 1954 (Picture: National Library of Australia)

The Queen visiting NASA at the beginning of the twenty-first century (Picture: NASA/Bill Ingalls)

105. Ripon Town Hall (Picture: Redvers)

House in the Rock, Knaresborough (Picture: Redvers)

Aldborough Manor. The village boasts a manor house as well as a hall. The listing information for this building states, 'Probably early C18, heightened, extended and refronted by R.N. Sharp in the mid C19.' Grade II listed (Picture: Alan Murray-Rust)

107. A view of Valley Gardens in 1900 (Picture: Library of Congress, LC-DIG-ppmsc-08423)

109. Battle Cross plaque. The reason for moving the cross from Boroughbridge to Aldborough is not explained in any source that I have found (Picture: Alan Murray-Rust)

111. Rowing boats trail their way along the River Nidd, with Knaresborough Castle in the background (Picture: TJ Blackwell at en.wikipedia)

Spofforth Castle (exterior) (Picture: Immanuel Giel)

113. Heatherdene at Harrogate District Hospital, the site of one of the Grand Duchess' hospitals, later demolished (Picture: akk7a)

The Grand Duchess (Picture: Library of Congress, George Grantham Bain Collection, LC-DIG-ggbain-17829)

115. Clapper Board (Picture: SXC)

117. Newby Hall (Picture: Andrew Whale)

119. Valley Gardens in 1900 (Picture: Library of Congress, LC-DIG-ppmsc-08424)

121. HM the Queen driving to St Paul's Cathedral during the Diamond Jubilee celebrations of 5 June 2012 (Picture: Carfax2)

123. The Whirlwind attraction at Lightwater Valley in action (Picture: Norms360)

Cherry blossom on The Stray (Picture: Fallen Tree Originals)

Swaledale sheep and dry-stone wall, Hebden, North Yorkshire (Picture: Alethe)

125. Prospect Hotel, now the Yorkshire Hotel, Prospect Place (Picture: Library of Congress, LC-DIG-ppmsc-08420)